USING SOCIAL PROOF IN YOUR BUSINESS

How to Unlock the Secret to Skyrocketing Sales
with Social Proof

by

EMERY V. BROWN

TABLE OF CONTENTS

WHAT IS SOCIAL PROOF?

Social proof is one of the most important things that you can use in your business. **Businesses that use social proof in their marketing and sales processes fare infinitely better than those that do not.**

But what exactly is social proof?

Imagine that you're browsing through Amazon, and you're looking for a new coffee table. You look through the hundreds of coffee tables that are offered through Amazon and you find a style and size that fits your needs.

You sort through these coffee tables and eventually you land on two coffee tables that you absolutely love:

- One of these tables has a rating of three out of five stars and 24 reviews.

- The other table has a rating of four out of five stars with over 300 reviews.

Which would you choose? It's a decision that almost doesn't need any further deliberation. You know exactly which table you're going to get. You're going to get the table that satisfies hundreds of other customers, who in fact, were so satisfied they decided to come back and leave a review of how good the product was.

This phenomenon is called social proof.

The term "social proof" is actually a relatively new term. It was first coined by Robert Cialdini in his book *Influence*.

In the broadest sense, social proof means that an individual will seek to copy or emulate the "acceptable" behavior of another individual that is undergoing or has undergone a similar situation.

If someone is in a situation that they've never been in before, like purchasing a new coffee table on Amazon, then they will naturally seek to copy the behavior of others who have done that thing before them.

This phenomenon also occurs when individuals in a group setting seek to conform their behavior to everyone else around them.

When it comes to marketing your business, social proof is used to make people feel comfortable in their purchasing decisions and to reinforce their belief that what they are doing is a good decision.

There are a whole host of ways to use social proof in your marketing, and we will be sure to cover those later in this guide.

Because social proof is so powerful, businesses all over the world strive to get reviews and testimonials from happy customers.

They know that seeing others happy with their products will encourage new customers to take the leap of faith and buy their products.

Why is Social Proof Important?

But why is social proof such a crucial and foundational pillar of marketing?

Consider these reasons:

- When people go online with the intent of buying something, they are very likely to look for reviews and testimonies from others who have used that product.

- Many shoppers ask their family and friends for recommendations before making a purchasing decision.

- Also, shoppers find new brands and new companies to buy from based upon the recommendations given to them by their family and friends.

There's no way around it. **Social proof and word-of-mouth marketing are two of the most powerful ways to market your business.** And it doesn't matter if you sell physical products, informational products, or anything in between.

Having social proof to back up your claims and to highlight your product is essential to the success of your business.

What Does Social Proof Look Like in Our Everyday Lives?

People look to other people when they are unsure of how they should act in any given social situation.

Remember earlier, when we mentioned the book *Influence* by Robert Cialdini?
This is a direct quote from that book:

"We are willing to place an enormous amount of trust in the collective knowledge of the crowd...Social Proof is most powerful for those who feel unfamiliar or unsure in a specific situation and who, consequently, must look outside themselves for evidence of how best to behave." - Robert Cialdini, Influence

And we see this played out every single day in our normal lives.

If we walk outside of a building and there's a large crowd of people looking up into the sky, what do we naturally want to do?

We want to look into the sky also. Not only because we're curious about what everyone else may be looking at but because we want to fit in with everyone else and not seem like an outcast.

In fact, it's been studied and observed that your brain will naturally take "Shortcuts" in order to speed up the decision-making process.

One of the shortcuts that your brain takes most often is the subconscious bias to follow the herd. And in this context, the herd is obviously the group of people looking upward.

Now that we have a better idea of what's going on with the social proof phenomenon, **let's look**

at some specific examples that we see every day:

1. **Bandwagon effect.** The first one that we're going to talk about is the bandwagon effect. One of the most obvious places that we see this effect happening is in sports.

   - Have you ever noticed that when a sports team starts doing really well and it looks like they're going to win it all, out of nowhere comes tons of supporters and secret fans of this team? This is nothing more than the bandwagon effect taking place.

   - **The bandwagon effect simply states that people are more likely to adopt certain behaviors and actions if the majority of a population are adopting those same behaviors and actions.**

- Other than sporting events, we also see this effect take place in political elections and humanitarian efforts.

2. **Social default bias.** This example of social proof simply states that without any outside forces acting on a person, **that person will naturally want to revert to the default or normal state that they usually find themselves in.**

   - A great example of the social default bias is when you're scrolling through your phone or downloading a new app and out of nowhere, you get hit with the terms and conditions for that app.

   - How many times have you actually made the effort to read through the terms and conditions and understand exactly what you're accepting?

- Probably not a whole lot. Because by doing that, you are imposing a lot of work and strain upon yourself and that would deviate from your "normal" at the moment.

When people resist the bandwagon effect or the social default bias, it usually causes a bit of a stir.

Two fantastic examples of people not succumbing to social default bias are:

- When Rosa Parks refused to give up her bus seat and helped spark the civil rights movement

- When the famous "Tank man" stood up to a convoy of tanks in Tiananmen Square

These social proofs and social biases are all around us at all times.

Learning the ins and outs of how people work within social situations gives you a tremendous advantage when you're marketing your business.

Which Businesses Benefit the Most from Social Proof?

Some newer business owners sometimes wonder if they need to rely on social proof as a chief aspect of their marketing. Some business owners think that their particular business in their particular offer cannot be helped by the presence of social proof.

This could not be further from the truth.

Every business could benefit from utilizing social proof. There are so many different ways to utilize social proof that can have such a profound effect on your business that it would be foolish not to do so.

In this guide, we're going to go into detail about exactly why social proof is essential to any business.

Let's briefly talk about what we'll be going over.

What You Will Learn

In this report:

- The first thing that we'll be covering is the psychology of social proof. We will be talking about why it's so effective and why every human is influenced by it.

- We'll look at the consequences of not using social proof in your business. And we will even cover how to use social proof even if your business is brand new.

- Following that, we'll dive into all the different types of social proof you can use in your business, from testimonials to case studies to celebrity endorsements.

- Once we have discussed different types of social proof, we will cover how to use and capitalize on this social proof in your business.

- And then to wrap everything up, we'll take a look at your next steps and what you can do to fully utilize social proof to increase the revenue of your business.

TH E PSYCHOLOGY OF SOCIAL PROOF

Social proof is a psychological tool just like reciprocity. It is a powerful and effective way to persuade your prospects to turn into customers.

But why exactly does it work so well?

Why do people always want to buy the product with 500 great reviews as opposed to the product with 30 mediocre reviews - even if the product with 30 mediocre reviews is better overall than the product with 500 reviews?

Being able to understand the psychology behind why social proof is so powerful will help you use those psychological principles in your business to further drive sales and communicate value and trust with your prospects.

Why It's So Effective

Ever since humans came onto the scene we have been programmed to adhere to the unspoken laws of social proof.

Consider these reasons:

1. **Humans, by their very nature, are social beings.** We naturally want to conform, whenever it is possible for us to do so.

   - Aristotle himself said that "Man is by nature social."

   - It's the reason that so many people are enthralled by social media and are disappointed in themselves if they don't "match up" with their friends and peers.

   - For example, if they see somebody on social media taking more vacations than them, they immediately feel inferior. If someone goes to the gym more than they do, they also feel inferior.

2. **Human beings want to conform to one another.** They want to stay within a very

narrow window of social "normalcy" and they don't want to stray very far from it.

- This is especially true when it comes to where someone will spend their hard-earned money.

- If you're walking down the street and you see two restaurants that look good but one of them has no line and the other restaurant has a line out the door, which would you automatically assume is better?

- Obviously, you're going to automatically think that the restaurant with a line out the door is the better restaurant. And that is because you want to conform to the social normalcy that is standing in the line with the others. Because they can't all be wrong about which restaurant is better.

3. **Humans have a deep desire to feel like they belong somewhere.** They want to feel like they belong to a certain tribe or a certain group.

   - This is why family is so important in most cultures.

   - This is why friendships are so important.

   - People generally don't want to be alone, facing the world without any support.

But what does this information mean to you?

It means you have one of the most primal and instinctual behaviors right at your fingertips, ready to be used to grow your business.

What Happens When You Don't Use Social Proof

Some businesses don't understand the value of social proof. They think that it's a nice addition to their marketing, but it's not essential to the success of their business. Luckily for you, you will not be falling into this category of business owner.

The business owner that doesn't understand social proof and who doesn't utilize it is doomed to fail.

Let's think about it like this: if you were really hungry and driving around looking for a restaurant to eat at, you probably wouldn't be too picky.

But let's say you drive up to a restaurant and when you look inside, you see that there's maybe one or two customers inside. Then you look up the restaurant online. You don't see any reviews by any previous customers and zero accreditations. Then you open up Yelp and try to search for the business, but you don't find anything about them.

How are you feeling about this restaurant now? Do you feel confident that this is going to be a pleasant dining experience? Or do you feel like it's going to be a gamble and that, more than likely, you're going to be disappointed?

Keep in mind, the business hasn't done anything to sway you at this point. Positive or negative. They simply lack any social proof. **And because they lack that social proof, your initial assessment of their business is negative.**

That's why using social proof is so important.

How You Can Use Social Proof Even if You're Just Starting Out

Using social proof for your business can seem like a catch 22 at the start. How do you use social proof to get new clients or customers when you haven't had any previous clients or customers?

Luckily, there is an easy way to get social proof of your business right at the very start.

In order to get the social proof that you need, you're going to use a different psychological trick.

And that trick is called: People really like free stuff.

No, but in all seriousness, this is how you get your first few examples of social proof.

This works particularly well with service-based businesses, but they can work with physical products as well.

Follow this process:

1. Reach out to four or five people who are in your target demographic.

2. Tell them that you're starting this new business and that you're trying to get it off the ground.

3. Because you're trying to get it off the ground, you would love to offer them your product or service for free. The only thing you'd like in return is a testimonial if they enjoy the service or product.

That's it! That's the whole strategy.

Yes, you'll be doing some work upfront without any pay. But **this is the quickest and easiest way to gather the social proof that you need.** And realistically, you won't be doing this for very long. You only need four or five pieces of social proof to seem like a credible source in your industry.

THE TYPES OF SOCIAL PROOF YOU SHOULD BE USING

So far, we've talked about why social proof is so important and why it's so effective at persuading people.

We also briefly touched on how to gather social proof if you don't have any already.

But now we need to talk about what that social proof looks like. In this next section, let's cover several different examples of how you can use social proof in your marketing.

Testimonials

Testimonials can come in a variety of formats, from text to audio and even video.

A testimonial is when a customer or a client has a positive experience with you, and they want to have it on record that they had a good experience with you.

Often, they will submit a piece of text or a video to let others, who are on the fence about purchasing your product or service, know that they had a good experience with you, and they recommend you.

Testimonials are fairly simple and straightforward. Because of this, they're not very hard to get. And if a customer has a truly great experience with you, they will usually be happy to supply you with one.

Out of all the different mediums that testimonials can come in, a video testimonial is typically the most powerful.

This is because video communicates emotions and builds trust better than text or audio alone. And since the name of the game with social proof is trust and credibility, video testimonials tend to work much better than any other form of testimonial.

Case Studies

Case studies are typically longer and more in-depth than the other types of social proof that we will be talking about.

A case study is a piece of social proof that tends to tell a story. This story is typically what happened when a specific customer or client had a problem, and you were able to solve the problem for the client.
Keep these points in mind:

1. **Tell an emotional story in your case study.** These case studies will have plenty of data and statistics to back up the story that they are telling. But with any kind of marketing, **stories and emotions typically sell better than logic and facts.**

   - So, in order to capitalize on that fact, you're going to want to tell a very emotional story of how the specific person or business had this problem, and without you, they never would've found a solution.

2. **Typically, you would want one or two case studies per offer that you provide.** You want a case study that seeks to relate to each client demographic that you have.

    - For example, if your business serves home contractors, then you want to have case studies of you working with plumbers, electricians, carpenters, and more.

Make sure you have a case study that can build rapport and persuade anyone in your target demographics!

Reviews

Reviews are on the other end of the spectrum from case studies. Case studies are typically longer pieces of content and usually you don't have a lot of them. However, **reviews are typically numerous and tend to be very short.**

Learn more about reviews:

- You will find reviews on service-based businesses. But most of the time you find reviews revolving around products, usually physical products.

- **A lot of the time these reviews take the form of a simple rating system.** You know, like on Amazon, how you can rate something from 1 to 5 stars. All of those ratings are reviews.

    - Sometimes those reviews will come with texts from the customers that made the reviews. That text segment of the review can almost be considered a testimonial. But the way in which it is used makes it a review.

- Typically, if you're going to use reviews for your products, you want to have a lot of reviews. Well-established businesses will have hundreds and sometimes even thousands of reviews for their products.

This is a great use of social proof. If you go onto a website to buy something, and you see that the product has thousands of happy customers that went back to review it, you're going to think much more highly of it than if it had no reviews at all.

Social Media

Social media can be a mixed bag for businesses.

If your social media is underutilized, it can be a huge missed opportunity for your business. But, **if used effectively, social media can be a fantastic channel for your business and can serve as a very lucrative means of social proof.**

With social media, you're going to be posting a lot of helpful content for your audience. You're also going to be interacting with your audience through comments and DM's.

And while these things are great at building your brand and getting new customers, it isn't exactly the social proof that we're looking for.

A lot of the social proof that we're looking for utilizes vanity metrics. These vanity metrics are things like the number of likes that a post receives or how many times your post was shared.

Remember back to the bandwagon effect?

If one post from a business on social media has thousands of likes and dozens and dozens of shares, someone who sees it for the first time is much more likely to pay attention and even give it a like themselves.

A lot of business gurus teach that these vanity metrics don't mean anything. And while they may not be as important as other metrics for your business, they should not be discarded entirely.

Gaining tons of new followers and amassing tons of engagement on social media helps to establish yourself as an authority and a credible source. It builds trust with your audience and plants the seed of social proof within them.

Celebrity Endorsements

Celebrity endorsements are another one of those weird and quirky psychological tricks that you can use within your marketing.

When you step back and think about it, it doesn't make a whole lot of sense as to why we assign such authority to celebrity figures, especially things like actors or musicians. And yet, millions of people look to these celebrities for their insights on things like politics, healthcare, and all other facets of society that they have nothing to do with.

But being the smart business owner that you are, you can see this phenomenon and take advantage of it.

Celebrity endorsements usually don't happen when you're a brand-new business, unless you have an outstanding product that is borderline revolutionary. Usually, the celebrity endorsement is a type of social proof that you get much later in the life of your business.

But once you're able to land a celebrity endorsement, you can use it as a type of social proof. **Once a celebrity endorses your service or your product, you achieve a new sense of perceived value from your target audience.**

See how celebrity endorsements work:

- Let's say, for example, that you sell a recording microphone for podcasters and voiceover artists. By itself, you'd probably do pretty well with this business.

- But what if you were to capture a video of Morgan Freeman using your microphone and telling people how wonderful it is?

- Instantly you're going to get an enormous amount of credibility and authority within your market, because others look at Morgan Freeman and his golden voice and assume that whatever he uses must be the top-of-the-line and the best available.

So, while a celebrity endorsement may be a ways away for you, it is definitely worth looking into when you're ready.

Expert Testimony

The expert testimony is a blend of two of the previously mentioned social proofs that we've talked about. **It's a combination of a regular testimonial and a celebrity endorsement.**

Because of that, you typically won't get expert testimony within the early stages of your business. But once you do get an expert testimony, it can be a fantastic asset for your business. Expert testimony is when a perceived expert or authority within your field approves of your product or service and even recommends it to their own following.

Here's an example of expert testimony with a product like kitchen knives:

- Let's say that you sell high-end kitchen knives. They're beautiful and high-quality stainless-steel knives and you have hundreds of reviews and testimonials from happy customers.

- Now that's awesome! You have a good product with good social proof behind it. You'll do very well.

- But let's imagine for a second that Gordon Ramsay gets in front of his huge audience and publicly endorses your knives. He says that they are the best knives he's ever used, and that he's going to be using your knives from now on in all of his kitchens.

- It's safe to assume that you will experience a tidal wave of new customers who want the knives that Gordon Ramsay himself is using.

Just like with the testimonial, a video expert testimony is going to be much more powerful than a testimonial in text.

And just like how a celebrity endorsement probably won't come along in the early stages of your business, expert testimony is a powerful piece of social proof that you can strive to get once your business has achieved some success.

WHERE TO PLACE SOCIAL PROOF FOR MAXIMUM EFFECTIVENESS

At this point, we've talked about what social proof is and why it is so powerful when you use it properly in your marketing.

We talked about the different types of social proof that you can use and how each one is slightly different from the other and the pros and cons of using them.

Now it's time to talk about what to do once you have the social proof.

Sales

Up until this point we've mostly talked about using social proof as a means of marketing your business.

But it is worth noting that **social proof can be incredibly powerful during the sales process** as well.

This mostly pertains to service-based businesses. With product-based businesses, most of the social proof will have already been delivered to the client through marketing.

But with service-based businesses, you often have to actually talk to your prospects. This can be an incredible opportunity to share the social proof with them in real-time.

During the course of your sales call, objections will come up. These objections are perfect places to interject case studies into your conversation. It does require that you have in-depth knowledge of all of your company's case studies so that you can pull from the right case studies for each prospect.

But being able to answer objections with actual case studies related to the objection that is being brought up could be an incredibly powerful way to move the sales conversation forward and further persuade the prospect to become a paying client.

Marketing

Most of our conversations so far have revolved around using social proof in your marketing. But where exactly, and in what marketing assets, do we place the social proof?

Place social proof in these venues:

1. **A**dvertisements. Social proof can be a fantastic thing to place in different advertisements around the web. From Facebook ads to Google ads to native advertisements, there are plenty of advertising avenues for you to place your social proof.

2. **Emails.** In addition to advertisements, your email list is also a fantastic place to share social proof. Email marketing has an insanely high ROI of at least 44X. This makes it one of the highest return marketing channels available to you.

- Share small, abbreviated versions of your case studies and testimonials with the people on your email list.

- Use strong copywriting skills and email list management skills in order to bring the most appropriate case studies and testimonials to your list.

3. **Blogs and other content marketing pieces.** In fact, entire pieces of content can revolve around specific pieces of social proof.

  - Audio and video marketing can be great when intertwined with social proof. **Interview current or previous customers** and get their specific take on working with you and the success that they have had.

4. **Landing and sales pages of your website.** In addition to all of that, having

social proof fill up the bottom of your landing pages and sales pages is always a smart move to help move those skeptical prospects along.

Your Website

Next, let's talk about how you can use social proof on your website. Using social proof on your website is a little bit more straightforward than in your sales and marketing.

Typically, your website is a pretty static asset. It generally stays the same for extended periods of time and isn't constantly evolving and moving like your sales and marketing will.

That being said, **it's always a good idea to have an entire page on your website devoted to nothing but testimonials, reviews, and case studies.**

Just like our other examples of where to put social proof, you want to make sure that there's a wide variety of case studies and social proof so that anybody who comes to your website with specific problems or objections can have them answered by your case studies and social proof.

Social Media

Put your social proof all over your social media. Social media audiences love seeing success and highlights.

Don't be afraid to share the different wins that your clients are experiencing as a result of working with you. Likewise, if you come across video reviews of your physical products, don't be afraid to share those on your social media.

However, this can be overdone. People don't want to think that you're just talking about your wild success every single time they log onto social media.

Post plenty of valuable content that helps to educate and inform your audience in addition to all of the social proof that you'll be putting in front of them as well.

NEXT STEPS

We've talked about exactly what social proof is and why it is so valuable to business owners.

We went behind the scenes and covered a lot of the psychology behind social proof and how it breaks down in the marketplace. We looked at a bunch of different types of social proof and how they can be applied in your business.

You have more than enough information now to go out and use social proof to strengthen and expand your business.

Even if you're brand new, you still have the ability to create compelling and persuasive social proof.

The number one secret to gathering insanely good social proof is to be really good at what you do and to ensure that you go above and beyond for your clients and customers. More social proof will naturally follow!

www.ingramcontent.com/pod-product-compliance
Lightning Source LLC
Chambersburg PA
CBHW040759240526
45474CB00008B/109